Joseph and the king of Egypt

Story by Penny Frank

Illustrated by Tony Morris

THE LION STORY BIBLE

8

TRING · BELLEVILLE · SYDNEY

The Bible tells us how God chose the Israelites to be his special people. He made them a promise that he would always love and care for them. But they must obey him.

This is the second part of the story of Joseph. Joseph's brothers had sold him as a slave because they were jealous of him.

They told Jacob, their father, that Joseph had been killed by a wild animal. But Joseph had been taken to Egypt.

You can find the story in your own Bible, in Genesis chapters 39 to 47.

Copyright © 1985 Lion Publishing

Published by
Lion Publishing plc
Icknield Way, Tring, Herts, England
ISBN 0 85648 733 3
Lion Publishing Corporation
10885 Textile Road, Belleville,
Michigan 48111, USA
ISBN 0 85648 733 3
Albatross Books
PO Box 320, Sutherland, NSW 2232, Australia
ISBN 0 86760 517 0

First edition 1985

Printed and bound in Hong Kong
by Mandarin Offset International (HK) Ltd

British Library Cataloguing in Publication Data
Frank, Penny
Joseph and the king of Egypt. –
(The Lion Story Bible; 8)
1. Joseph *(Biblical patriarch)* –
Juvenile literature
2. Bible stories, English – O.T.
Genesis
I. Title   II. Series
222'.110924   BS580.J6

ISBN 0-85648-733-3

Library of Congress Cataloging in Publication Data
Frank, Penny.
Joseph and the king of Egypt.
(The Lion Story Bible; 8)
1. Joseph (Sons of Jacob)—Juvenile literature. 2. Bible. O.T.—Biography—Juvenile literature. [1. Joseph (Son of Jacob) 2. Bible stories—O.T.] I. Morris, Tony, ill. II. Title. III. Series: Frank, Penny. Lion Story Bible; 8.
BS580.J6F728 1985   222'.1109505
84-25034
ISBN 0-85648-733-3

Joseph lived in a land called Egypt.
But his real home was in Canaan, where
his family lived. There he had a father
called Jacob, who loved him very much.
He also had eleven brothers.

Joseph found his new life very hard.
In Canaan he had been the son his
father, Jacob, loved most.

Here in Egypt people stared at him,
because he came from another country.
  'You can see he's not one of us,'
they said.

In Canaan he had been able to have everything he wanted, because his father was rich.

In Egypt he had been sold to a rich man. He was a slave. But he did his work so well that before long he had an important job. He had to look after the rich man's house.

God had not forgotten Joseph. But he wanted Joseph to change. He did not want him to be a spoiled boy who got his brothers into trouble.

He wanted Joseph to trust him and to become a man other people could trust.

One day Joseph was put in prison for something he had not done. Even in prison God helped him.

The prison was horrible. It was dark and smelly.

The jailer saw how hard Joseph worked. So he put him in charge of all the other prisoners.

Joseph made friends with the prisoners.
When two of them had puzzling dreams,
Joseph helped them.

'God will tell me what the dreams
mean,' he said, and he explained them.

'In three days' time you will be set free,' he said to one of the men. 'Please don't forget to ask someone to let me out too.'

This man's job was to bring wine to the king himself.

Sure enough, he was set free and worked for the king, just as Joseph had said.

But two years passed and Joseph was
still in prison. Then the king had a
dream, and the man remembered Joseph.

'I know someone who can explain
your dream,' he said to the king. 'His
God helps him.'

So the king sent for Joseph.

'I have had a very strange dream,' he said. 'My servant says you can explain it.'

'My God will help me,' said Joseph.

The king dreamed he was standing by the great river of Egypt.

He saw seven fat cows come out of the
water and start to eat the grass.

Then he saw seven skinny cows come
out of the water. They ate up the
seven fat cows but stayed as thin
as before.

'I wish I knew what it meant,' he cried.

Joseph told the king, 'God wants you to know that there are going to be seven years when we will all have plenty of food to eat. But you must save some of the food, because for seven years after that there will not be enough.'

'I am glad God told us,' said the king.
'We must store up all the food we can.
    'We shall need someone in charge.
I think that you should do it.'

So Joseph became the most important man in Egypt. He stored up the food when there was plenty.

Then, when there was no harvest, the people came to buy food from him.

People came from other lands to buy
food too. Even in Canaan, where Joseph's
father lived, the harvests were poor
and the people were very hungry.

One day, when Joseph was busy in the
storehouse, he saw his own brothers
coming through the door. They did not
know this great man was Joseph.
And he did not tell them right away.
First he wanted to find out if they
were still as cruel.

When he knew they had really changed, Joseph told them who he was. They were very ashamed.

But Joseph said, 'Please don't be sad. Look how God has cared for me. Go and bring Jacob, my father. I want you all to come and live with me in Egypt. There are five more hungry years to come.'

Jacob had been so sure that Joseph was dead. How glad he was to see him again!

He was happy to live in Egypt, where there was plenty of food.

The Lion Story Bible is made up of 52 individual stories for young readers, building up an understanding of the Bible as one story — God's story — a story for all time and all people.

The Old Testament section (numbers 1–30) tells the story of a great nation — God's chosen people, the Israelites — and God's love and care for them through good times and bad. The stories are about people who knew and trusted God. From this nation came one special person, Jesus Christ, sent by God to save all people everywhere.

The story of *Joseph and the king of Egypt* comes from the first book of the Old Testament, Genesis chapters 39 to 47. It tells how Joseph learned to trust God in his troubles and how God took care of him. It was God who made sure that when famine came Joseph was in a position to save his family — God's people — from starvation. The story also shows how Joseph's cruel brothers changed for the better. These twelve sons of Jacob were the founders of the twelve tribes of Israel.

The next story in the series, number 9: *The princess and the baby* tells how the people of Israel became slaves in Egypt, and of God's plan to rescue them.

Most of all, Jacob was glad that Joseph
was a man who could be trusted. God
had changed him, and he had changed
the cruel brothers.

Jacob thanked God for taking care
of Joseph in Egypt.